D0845271

EDGE
BOOKS™

WARRIORS OF HISTORY

Knights

by Michael Martin

Consultant:
Dr. Miri Rubin
Professor of European History
University of London

Capstone
press

Mankato, Minnesota

Edge Books are published by Capstone Press,
151 Good Counsel Drive, P.O. Box 669, Mankato, Minnesota 56002.
www.capstonepress.com

Library of Congress Cataloging-in-Publication Data
Martin, Michael, 1948–
    Knights/by Michael Martin.
    p. cm.—(Edge Books. Warriors of History)
    ISBN-13: 978-0-7368-6431-2 (hardcover)
    ISBN-10: 0-7368-6431-8 (hardcover)
    1. Knights and knighthood—Europe—Juvenile literature. 2. Civilization,
Medieval—Juvenile literature. I. Title. II. Series.
CR4513.M38 2007
940.1—dc22   2005034930

Summary: Describes medieval knights, including their history, weapons,
and way of life.

Editorial Credits
Mandy Robbins, editor; Thomas Emery, designer; Cynthia Martin, illustrator;
    Kim Brown, production colorist; Jo Miller, photo researcher; Scott Thoms,
    photo editor

Photo Credits
Art Directors/Brian Gibbs, 29
The Bridgeman Art Library/Private Collection/Ken Welsh, 22–23; Staatsbibliothek,
    Berlin Germany/Giraudon, 4
Corbis/Andrew Fox, 28; Bettmann, 13, 16–17, 18, 26–27; Darama, cover
The Granger Collection, New York, 6–7, 11
Mary Evans Picture Library, 8, 9, 14, 24
Private Collection/Ken Welsh/The Bridgeman Art Library, 22–23

397 0566

1 2 3 4 5 6 11 10 09 08 07 06

TABLE OF CONTENTS

CHAPTER 1

The Age of Knighthood

Learn About:
- *Warriors of the Middle Ages*
- *Chivalry*
- *Sieges and Crusades*

Medieval battles were full of the sounds of clanging metal. Knights fought with swords, axes, and other heavy metal tools.

Battles during the Middle Ages were violent, bloody affairs. Arrows hissed through the air. Foot soldiers hacked and stabbed with swords and daggers. The most deadly fighters were knights. These armored warriors thundered into battle on horseback. From AD 800 to 1400, knights were the best combat force in Europe.

Back then, Europe was made up of about 15 kingdoms. Each kingdom was divided into lordships. Lords constantly struggled to keep control of their property. They needed strong armies to protect their land.

Knights were the most important members of any European army. As their lords' most dedicated defenders, they were seen as heroes.

A warhorse was a knight's most expensive piece of equipment. A good one cost more than most people earned in a lifetime.

Kings and lords often led their knights into battle.

ELITE FIGHTERS

The path to knighthood was not open to everyone. Knights had to buy their own battle gear. Horses, weapons, and armor cost a lot of money. Poor peasants and serfs could not afford to be knights. For these reasons, knights almost always came from the wealthiest classes of medieval society.

CODE OF CONDUCT

Being a knight was more than a job. It was a way of life. Knights lived by a set of rules called chivalry. According to these rules, knights were guardians of the Christian religion. They had to be polite to women and honest in all their dealings. Not all knights lived up to these standards. But most would risk their lives to obey these rules.

Chivalry demanded that a knight be respectful of women and protect the innocent.

It was a knight's duty to obey and protect his master's land and the people in it.

DUTY AND DANGER

Whenever one kingdom attacked another, knights were called to action. They sometimes fought for months to capture or defend a castle.

Knights were also the most fearsome warriors in battles called Crusades. During these battles, knights traveled to faraway countries to win lands controlled by non-Christians.

EDGE FACT

Knights joined Crusades for more than the opportunity to spread their religion. Crusades offered adventure, travel, and the chance to use their fighting skills.

Knights of the Crusades formed Christian brotherhoods. They wore cloaks with colored crosses to show which group they belonged to.

CHAPTER II
The Life of a Knight

Knights usually lived in castles or manor houses. Lords gave them land and serfs to raise animals and crops. In return, the knights protected the lords' land and castles.

Training for knighthood began early. A son of a knight or nobleman was sent to a different castle at the age of 7. There, he served as a page. Pages learned manners and how to obey orders.

Around age 14, a page became a squire. As a knight's personal attendant, he tended to his master's horse, weapons, and armor. Squires traveled with knights when they went into battle.

Squires had to be physically strong to become knights. They spent many hours learning how to control a powerful horse and use heavy weapons.

Learn About:

- Pages and squires
- Bloody battles
- Jousting

Serfs lived and worked on a knight's land. They were treated like slaves.

If a squire fought well enough to survive a battle, he was usually made an official knight.

A KNIGHT AT LAST

In rare cases, a squire might be called to battle. If he showed bravery, the squire could become a knight on the battlefield. But usually it took four years of training to become a knight. Most squires became knights through a special ceremony called "dubbing."

When a squire was dubbed, he swore an oath to serve his lord. Then, a king, queen, or another knight tapped him on the shoulders with a sword. At that moment, the squire became a knight.

A GRUESOME JOB

Medieval battles were brutal and bloody. Much of the fighting was done with swords and razor-sharp axes. It was common for arms, legs, and even heads to be cut off during combat.

Godfrey of Bouillon was a famous knight. He lopped off the heads of many enemies with his sharp sword. During one battle, he performed a feat that became legendary. He took a mighty swing at an enemy approaching on horseback. Godfrey's sword cut the man completely in half. The part of the enemy's body above the waist fell to the ground. The part below the waist stayed in the saddle as the horse galloped away.

Jousting was a deadly sport at early medieval tournaments.

FIGHTING FOR FUN

During times of peace, knights showed their skills at competitions called tournaments. Jousting was the most popular event. In jousting, two knights rode toward each other carrying spears called lances. Knights used lances to try to knock each other off their horses.

EDGE FACT

The first tournaments were much like real battles. Teams of 40 or more knights attacked each other in fights that could last all day.

The first tournaments were nearly as dangerous as actual wars. At a tournament in Cologne in 1240, 60 knights were killed. So many knights were killed during jousting that special tournament lances were made. They had wooden tips that would wound, but not kill, a contestant.

CHAPTER III

A Knight's Necessities

Learn About:
- *Arrows and armor*
- *Warhorses*
- *Most important weapon*

Knights had to have their shields ready at all times to guard against the swords, spears, and arrows that came at them.

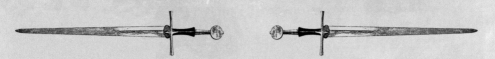

The key to a knight's success was his equipment. The earliest knights wore chain mail shirts. Chain mail was made by tightly hooking metal rings together. Even the sharpest swords had trouble cutting through it.

Knights wore padding underneath their chain mail. It protected them from the blows of battle hammers and heavy clubs called maces. These weapons could crush bones or knock a man senseless.

ARMOR

By the 1400s, some knights wore suits of armor. Armor was made of metal plates that covered a knight's body. A suit of armor often weighed 50 pounds (23 kilograms) or more. It was so heavy that some knights needed help mounting their horses.

Sword
Medieval swords could range in length from 2 to 6 feet (.6 to 1.8 meters) long.

Shield
The wealthiest knights had shields made of metal. Poorer knights used wooden shields.

Helmet
Some helmets had only a noseguard, while others had metal visors that covered the entire face.

Coat of arms
Knights displayed their family symbols on their shields and armor.

Armor
An entire suit of metal-plated armor weighed between 40 and 60 pounds (18 to 27 kilograms).

WARHORSES AND WEAPONS

The knight's warhorse was his most valuable piece of equipment. Some knights even fitted their horses with armor. Strong, obedient horses were the most desirable. They were trained to step on or over the bodies of fallen soldiers.

Knights galloped toward their enemies with their lances pointed straight ahead, ready to attack. Knights carried other weapons too. Some used a mace for close fighting. A mace had a ball with metal spikes on one end. The metal spikes smashed through armor. Other weapons included axes, hammers, and pointed daggers.

A sword was a knight's most important weapon. The longsword was the most popular sword. Its long blade was sharp on both sides. It was heavy enough to split armor. Greatswords were even heavier. They weighed as much as 20 pounds (9 kilograms). The blade of a greatsword could easily slice off an arm or leg.

Knights were the armored tanks of their day. A hard-charging group of knights could crush everything in its path. Knights rode side by side. Together, each horse and rider weighed nearly 2,000 pounds (900 kilograms). Enemies on foot could not stand up to that kind of power.

KNIGHTS ON FOOT

Knights were sometimes forced to fight on foot. If a knight was knocked off his horse in battle, he was in great danger. His heavy armor slowed him down.

Castle invasions were brutal affairs. Attackers often had boulders and hot oil dropped on their heads.

During a castle invasion, knights were forced to fight on foot as well. This often involved climbing castle walls while enemies shot blazing arrows at them.

Armor was not the only piece of equipment that slowed a knight down. Helmets made it difficult for knights to see where they were going. One story tells of a knight who was climbing a ladder up a wall around a city. Halfway up the ladder, he took off his helmet to see where he was going. At that moment, an arrow sliced through his head. It killed him instantly.

CHAPTER IV

The End of an Age

Learn About:

- Gunpowder
- A new way of fighting
- Mercenaries

The introduction of cannons and guns marked the beginning of the end for knights.

Knighthood began to fade during the 1400s and 1500s. The invention of deadly new weapons was to blame. Gunpowder was most responsible for ending the age of knights.

Guns, muskets, and cannons were common on European battlefields by the late 1400s. In 1494, a group of Italy's finest knights attacked French soldiers. The French soldiers had spent far less time in military training than the knights had. Yet the knights were mowed down by a hail of musket balls.

Such battles made it clear that guns had changed the future of war. Knights, no matter how brave, were no match for the explosive force of gunpowder.

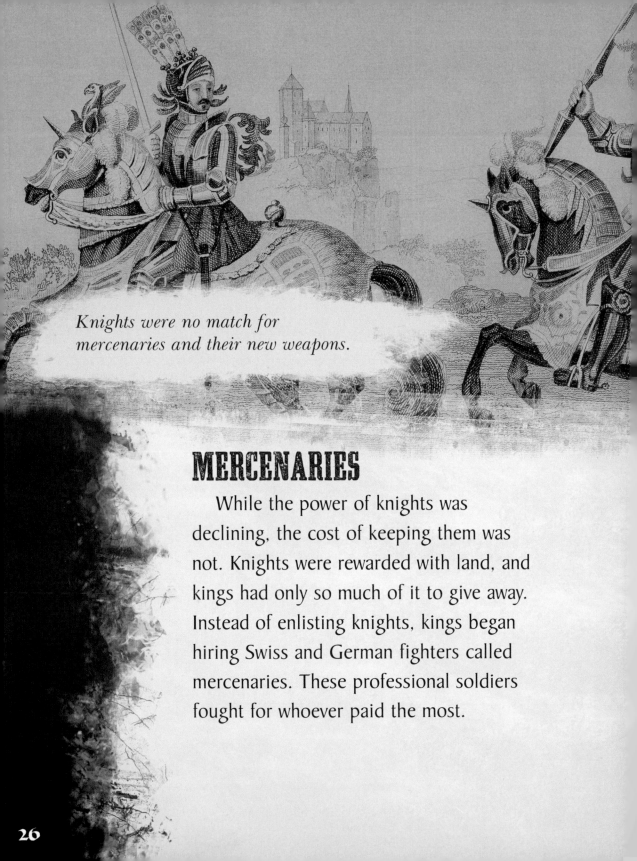

Knights were no match for mercenaries and their new weapons.

MERCENARIES

While the power of knights was declining, the cost of keeping them was not. Knights were rewarded with land, and kings had only so much of it to give away. Instead of enlisting knights, kings began hiring Swiss and German fighters called mercenaries. These professional soldiers fought for whoever paid the most.

Gunpowder was not the only threat to knights. By 1370, crossbows fired arrows that could pierce armor.

Mercenaries used firearms and long poles called pikes to defeat knights. Pikes could knock knights completely off their horses. Once on the ground, knights were finished off with muskets or handguns. The use of mercenaries made it even clearer that the age of knighthood was over.

People dress up and reenact life in the
Middle Ages at Renaissance festivals held
around the world.

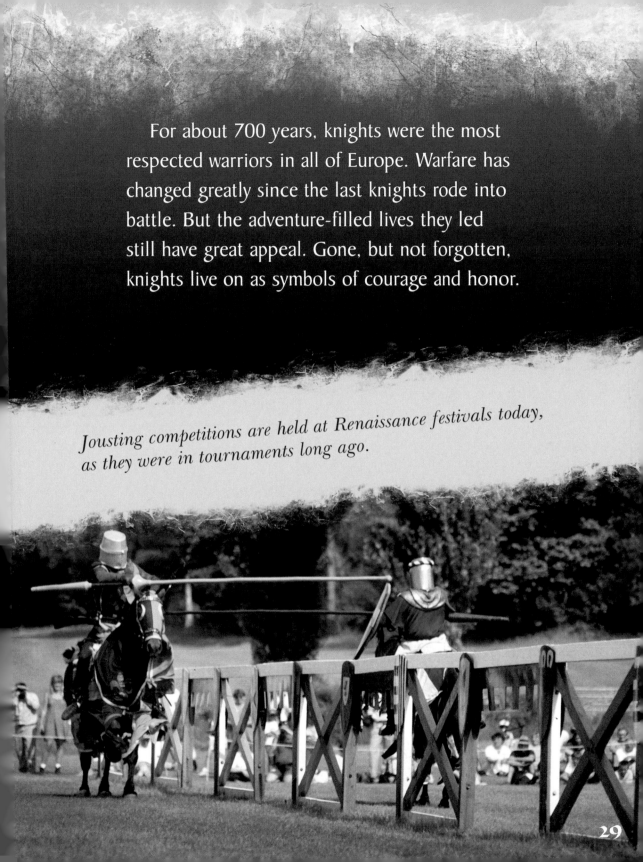

For about 700 years, knights were the most respected warriors in all of Europe. Warfare has changed greatly since the last knights rode into battle. But the adventure-filled lives they led still have great appeal. Gone, but not forgotten, knights live on as symbols of courage and honor.

Jousting competitions are held at Renaissance festivals today, as they were in tournaments long ago.

Index